COOLCOMPETITIONS

Astonishing
ROBOT
COMPETITIONS

BY JOHN R. BAKER

CAPSTONE PRESS
a capstone imprint

Blazers Books are published by Capstone Press,
1710 Roe Crest Drive, North Mankato, Minnesota 56003
www.mycapstone.com

Library of Congress Cataloging-in-Publication
Names: Baker, John R. (John Ronald), 1989– author.
Title: Astonishing robot competitions / by John R. Baker.
Description: Mankato, Minnesota : Capstone Press, [2018] | Series: Blazers.
   Cool competitions | Audience: Age 8-12. | Audience: Grade 4 to 6. |
   Includes bibliographical references and index.
Identifiers: LCCN 2017002059 (print) | LCCN 2017012094 (ebook) |
   ISBN 9781515773528 (library binding) | ISBN 9781515773566 (eBook PDF)
Subjects: LCSH: Robotics—Competitions—Juvenile literature. |
   Robots—Juvenile literature.
Classification: LCC TJ211.2 (ebook) | LCC TJ211.2 .B354 2018 (print) |
   DDC 629.8/92—dc23
LC record available at https://lccn.loc.gov/2017002059

Summary: Describes various types of robots and robot competitions held around
the world.

Editorial Credits
Aaron Sautter, editor; Kyle Grenz, designer; Eric Gohl, media researcher;
Steve Walker, production specialist

Photo Credits
Alamy: US Navy Photo, 12; Newscom: AFLO/Rodrigo Reyes Marin, 27, picture-
alliance/dpa/Sebastian Willnow, 21, Xinhua News Agency/Li Changxiang,
7, ZUMA Press/Robin Nelson, 8; RoboGames.net: Alan Musselman, 17, Ariel
Zambelich, 15, Dave Schumaker, 22–23, 28–29, R-TEAM Robotics, 24, Sam
Coniglio, 5, 18; Shutterstock: phipatbig, cover (right), Roman Sotola, cover (left);
Stefan Hrabar/CSIRO: 11

Printed and bound in China.
0517/CA21700460 042017 004883

TABLE OF CONTENTS ▶

BRING ON THE ROBOTS!

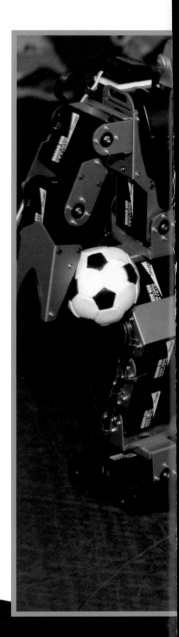

Robots are useful in many ways. They can help clean homes, build cars, or grow crops. Some even explore space. But robots can also be a lot of fun. Many people like to show off their robots in competitions around the world.

robot—a machine programmed to do jobs usually performed by a person

autonomous—able to control oneself; autonomous robots are not controlled by a person

AND THE WINNER IS...

▶ People **program** robots to do many actions. In skill challenges, competitors build robots to do tasks quickly and accurately. They then compete to see which robot will win.

program—to enter a series of step-by-step instructions into a computer or robot that tells it what to do

engineer—someone trained to design and build things

Many schools and businesses hold robot competitions. They hope to encourage students to become scientists and **engineers**.

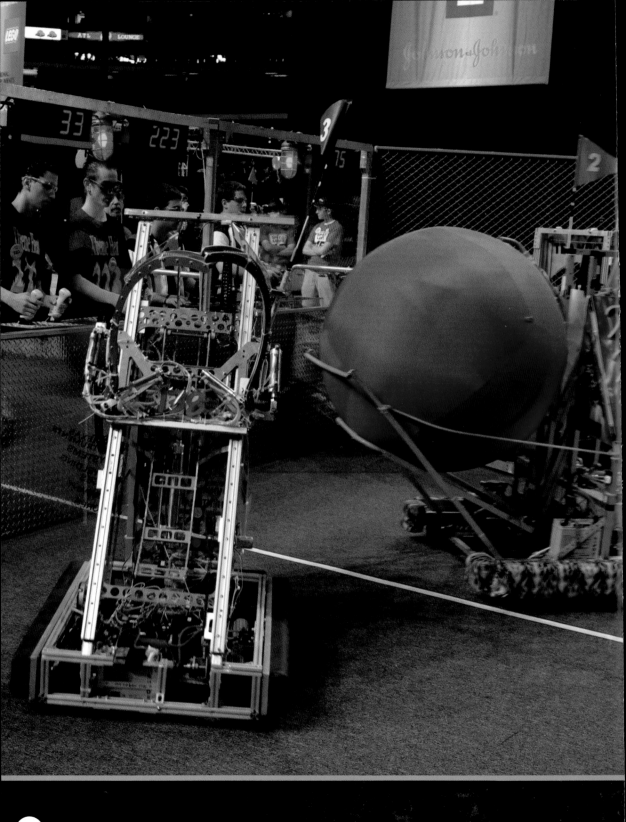

FIRST Competition

The FIRST competition features teams of student robot designers. Students build robots to solve problems or complete jobs. The robots may need to stack objects or shoot balls at a goal. Teams win by earning the most points.

FACT

In the 2017 FIRST competition, robots earned points by collecting parts to build an airship.

UAV Challenge-Outback Rescue

The **UAV** Challenge-**Outback** Rescue is held each year in Australia. In this event, teams fly unmanned robotic aircraft. They compete to find a **mannequin** in the wilderness. They also try to drop supplies as close to it as possible.

UAV—unmanned aerial vehicle; a robotic aircraft piloted by remote control

outback—the flat desert areas of Australia; few people live in the outback

mannequin—a life-sized model of a human

The winning team of the Outback Rescue
challenge receives a $50,000 (AU) grand prize.

In 2014 the MUROC DareDivas team won first
place in the Airborne Delivery Challenge.

FACT

Elementary school students can also compete at RoboSub. They build SeaPerch robots that explore under water.

Robosub

Teams of high school and college students take robots underwater in the RoboSub contest. The robots earn points by travelling through **obstacles** and firing **torpedoes**. The team with the most points in the finals wins.

obstacle—something that gets in the way or blocks progress

torpedo—an underwater missile

National Robotics Challenge

The National Robotics Challenge (NRC) is open to students from sixth grade through college. Students can compete in 13 different categories. They build manufacturing robots, rescue robots, combat robots, and more.

THE THRILL OF VICTORY

The contestants race, kick, and punch as they compete. But these athletes aren't human — they're robots. They compete with gears, wheels, and metal **limbs**. Like at any sporting event, robot fans cheer for their favorites.

limb—a part of the body used in moving or grasping; arms and legs are limbs

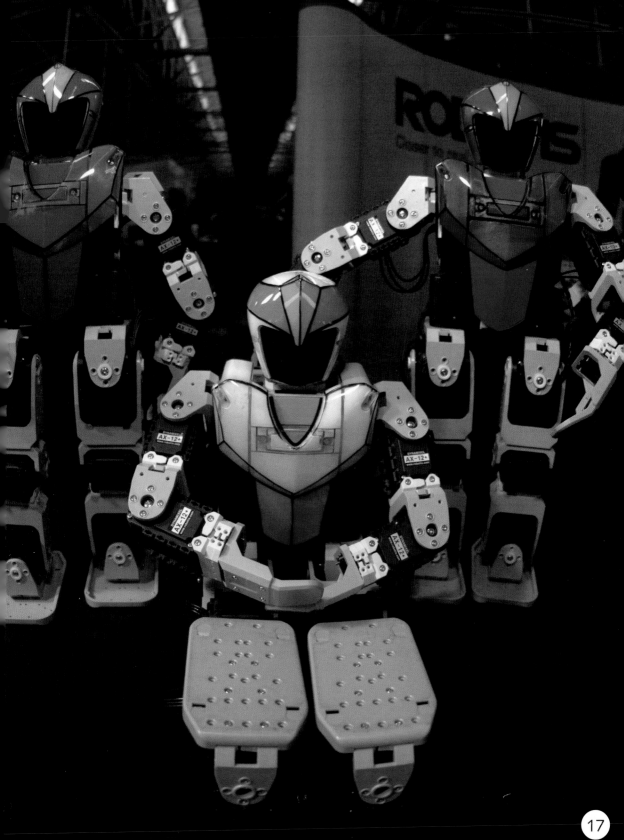

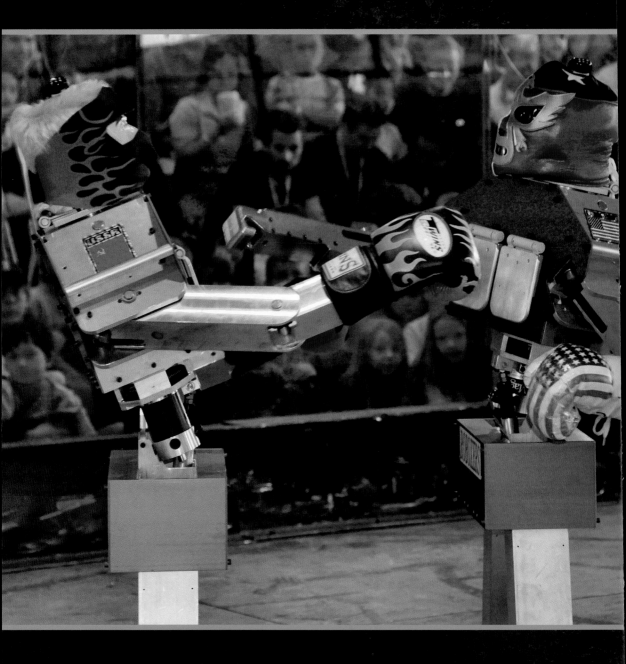

Robogames

The Robogames is like the Olympics for robots. Robots may compete in weightlifting, boxing, street hockey, and many other events. **Humanoid** robots also compete in soccer matches.

humanoid—having human form or characteristics; a humanoid robot is shaped somewhat like a human

RoboCup Soccer

Each year, teams from around the world compete in the RoboCup soccer **tournament**. It includes both rolling and humanoid robots. Rolling robots push a ball around the play area. Humanoid robots walk, run, and kick a ball like people do.

tournament—a series of matches between several players or teams, ending with one winner

RoboCup organizers hope that robots can compete against human soccer players by 2050.

CLASH OF THE BOTS

▶ Smash! Crash! Crunch! Sparks fly during robot battles. Teams create the fastest and toughest robots they can. They build robots with spinning saws, smashing hammers, and grasping claws. It's time for a robot rumble!

The first major robot battle took place at the Critter Crunch in 1989. The winning robot defeated the others while spraying a can of Silly String.

FACT

Robots in Mech Warfare face off in miniature models of cities.

Mech Warfare

At the Robogames, one popular event is Mech Warfare. Robots may have up to six legs. They fight with mini **flamethrowers**, mini rockets, and other weapons. The last robot standing wins.

flamethrower—a weapon that shoots a stream of burning liquid

Wrestling Bots

In Japan, FujiSoft, Inc. hosts the FSI-All Japan Robot Sumo Tournament each year. The battles are like sumo matches. The robots score points by pushing their opponents out of the ring. The first robot to win two out of three matches wins.

If a sumo robot tips over, it is allowed to right itself if it's still inside the ring.

BattleBots

In BattleBots, arenas are filled with fire, saw blades, and floor spikes. Tough robots try to destroy their opponents. They fight for three minutes or until one can't move. Teams keep battling until one is named the champion.

FACT

Losing BattleBot teams have one more chance to show off their robots. During the Robot Rumble, each robot tries to disable as many opponents as possible.

Glossary

autonomous (aw-TAH-nuh-muhss)—able to control oneself;
autonomous robots are not controlled by a person

engineer (en-juh-NEER)—someone trained to design and build things

flamethrower (FLAYM-throh-ur)—a weapon that shoots a stream of
burning liquid

humanoid (HYOO-muh-noyd)—having human form or characteristics;
a humanoid robot is shaped somewhat like a human

limb (LIM)—a part of the body used in moving or grasping; arms and
legs are limbs

mannequin (MAN-ih-kin)—a life-sized model of a human

obstacle (OB-stuh-kuhl)—something that gets in the way or
blocks progress

outback (OUT-back)—the flat desert areas of Australia; few people
live in the outback

program (PROH-gram)—to enter a series of step-by-step instructions
into a computer or robot that tells it what to do

robot (ROH-bot)—a machine programmed to do jobs usually
performed by a person

torpedo (tor-PEE-doh)—an underwater missile

tournament (TUR-nuh-muhnt)—a series of matches between several
players or teams, ending with one winner

UAV—unmanned aerial vehicle; a robotic aircraft piloted
by remote control

Read More

Clay, Kathryn. *Battling for Victory: The Coolest Robot Competitions*. The World of Robots. North Mankato, Minn.: Capstone Press, 2014.

Swanson, Jennifer. *Everything Robotics: All the Photos, Facts, and Fun!* National Geographic Kids Everything. Washington, D.C.: National Geographic, 2016.

Tuchman, Gail. *Robots*. Scholastic Reader, Level 2. New York: Scholastic Inc., 2016.

Internet Sites

Use FactHound to find Internet sites related to this book.

Visit *www.facthound.com*

Just type in 9781515773528 and go.

Check out projects, games and lots more at
www.capstonekids.com

Index